Echoes of the Soul

Copyright © 2024 by Jacqueline Gordon

All rights reserved.

Permission to reproduce or transmit in any form or by any means, electronic or mechanical, including photocopying, photographic and recording audio or video, or by any information storage and retrieval system, must be obtained in writing from the author.

Visit soulechoes.org for more information.

Echoes of the Soul is a registered trademark of Jacqueline Gordon.

First printing June 2024

Paperback ISBN: 9798329196436

Published by Royal Palms Publishing, LLC
Eva Myrick, MSCP, Publisher
info@royalpalmspublishing.com

Printed in the U.S.A.

Echoes of the Soul

LIVE IN YOUR HEALING JOURNAL

Seeking a connection with our inner selves can lead to a deeper understanding of who we are and what truly matters to us. It can be a journey of self-discovery and growth. How do you currently strive to connect with your inner self? Think of hearing the words *Echoes of the Soul* as we navigate through self-reflective exercises. You many find that you feel quite profound. It suggests a sense of seeking resonance with our deepest desires and truths. Here you can tap into your innermost thoughts, feelings, and desires. In those moments of introspection, we can connect with ourselves on a deeper level and gain insight into what truly matters. This self-awareness can lead to personal growth, clarity, and a greater sense of alignment with our values and aspirations.

~Jacqueline Gordon

~Jacqueline Gordon

About Me

I value my resilience and strength in facing and working through the traumas I have experienced throughout my life. Healing from past wounds is a courageous journey, and it is important for me to acknowledge the progress I have made. Someone very special once told me, "You are not alone on this journey, and I believe in your ability to heal and find peace within yourself."

I have yearned for a connection with my inner self my whole life. It has been a profound and powerful journey to undertake. I learned that seeking this connection through self-reflection, introspection, mindfulness practices, and other creative outlets has been incredibly rewarding. For me, it is a journey of self-discovery and self-awareness that has led to greater clarity, purpose, and fulfillment in life. I am not done.

Understandably, longing for a connection with your inner self can lead you down various paths in search of fulfillment and understanding. Sometimes, we try different things in hopes of finding that sense of connection and belonging. Each experience, whether positive or challenging, can offer valuable lessons and insights that ultimately contribute to our growth and self-discovery.

Embrace the journey through journaling as a process of learning and exploration. Trust that you will find the connection you seek within yourself. Remember to be compassionate with yourself as you continue to navigate your path of healing through journaling. Seeking support from therapists, support groups, or other resources can also be beneficial in your healing process. You are not alone.

"Write" your way to emotional healing or "Right" your way.

~Jacqueline Gordon

This journal is a tool to help you through your healing journey. Use it in a way that feels right for you.

Let's begin!

TABLE OF CONTENTS

INTRODUCTION

CHAPTER ONE: There's More?

CHAPTER TWO: Thirsty

CHAPTER THREE: Almost

CHAPTER FOUR: Sadness

CHAPTER FIVE: God's Grace

Choosing to "write" your way to freedom implies that personal growth, self-expression, and emotional release can come from engaging in writing. It suggests your willingness to explore and understand yourself through creativity and self-reflection.

On the other hand, choosing to be "right" about everything implies a stubbornness or rigidity in your beliefs, often at the cost of your personal well-being or relationships. Insisting on always being "right" can lead to conflict, isolation, and lack of growth or understanding.

Ultimately, the choice between the two is about "writing" as a way toward freedom. This happens by prioritizing personal growth, self-awareness, and emotional freedom over always needing to be "right." It encourages embracing the vulnerability and self-discovery that "writing" can offer.

~Jacqueline Gordon

INTRODUCTION

This journal is designed to be your companion on a path of healing and self-discovery. Throughout its pages, you will find prompts, activities, and reflections that will help you explore past experiences, process difficult emotions, and ultimately find peace and acceptance.

What to Expect:

Five Chapters: This journal is divided into five chapters, each one focusing on a different aspect of the healing process. These chapters will guide you through steps like:

- Understanding Your Pain: Reflecting on the root causes of your emotional pain and how it manifests in your life.
- Forgiving Others: Exploring forgiveness for those who have hurt you.
- Finding Strength: Discovering your own inner strength and resilience.
- Embracing Grace: Finding peace and acceptance through self-forgiveness and the concept of grace (if that resonates with you).
- Reflective Questions: Each chapter will begin with a series of reflective questions designed to help you delve deeper into your thoughts and feelings.
- Activities: Following the questions, you will find activities that can help you process your emotions and move forward. Some activities may be creative, such as writing a letter or creating a collage. Others may be more introspective, such as journaling exercises or meditations.
- Affirmations: Each chapter will conclude with an affirmation, a positive statement that you can repeat to yourself to cultivate self-compassion and encourage growth.

What I Won't Do:

- Tell You What To Feel: This journal is not designed to duplicate your healing process. Your emotions are valid, and there is no right or wrong way to feel.

- Offer One-Size-Fits-All Solutions: Everyone's healing journey is unique. This journal provides a framework, but ultimately you are in charge of your healing.

Remember:

- Be patient with yourself. Healing is not a linear process, and there will be challenges along the way. Take your time, do not write or try to heal in haste.

- Be kind to yourself. Treat yourself with compassion and understanding.

- Celebrate your progress. Acknowledge the steps you have taken, even the small ones.

> "Our wounds are often the openings into the best and most beautiful parts of us"
>
> – David Kessler

CHAPTER ONE: There's More?

Catapulted into a new dimension,
surrounded by your words that somehow apply to unheard truths to be told now as we make a path for me to heal.
I am screaming, see my tears?
It is not time to rejoice?
Between cries, laughter, anger, poise, even silent screams,
you have given me a voice,
my choice to use our space.
I want now more than ever before to seize each moment.
Never-ending desire to hear your voice against my ears
as my mind races to find its place – it's not my fault.
Driven by more than a dozen fears – destined to self-destruct,
emotional bombs exploding but I am holding.
Aching for the solace in your words, your demeanor, your genuineness,
your heart, your loyalty.
You cared – so you brought – what I needed, what I sought.
Your interpretation of my mental processes,
you opened a space for me to explore
the unconscious content lying in my mind, and at my body's inside door.
Why not use my voice to open my consciousness?
Because now I have a choice.
You'd say - in a psychodynamic way.
We will make time for you to convey
empathy heard when you spoke.
Pain felt as my pain moved around in the stillness of my thoughts
still clinging to my defenses, but no mention of what's broke.
A new me is rising to be,
more time is needed to remove another mask.
You have prepared me making me suited for the task.
Please not without you by my side.

I Am Who I Was Waiting For.
~Jacqueline Gordon

Now that you have finished reading chapter one, "There's More," it is time to confront your past. Read and reflect on the following carefully. Write down your answers in the spaces provided below.

The entry **"THERE'S MORE"** starts with being "catapulted into a new dimension." What event(s) in your past brought about this feeling of significant change?

_____

_____

_____

_____

The line "safely comforted – It's not my fault" suggests a burden of blame. Who or what do you feel responsible for, and how does this impact your life?

_____

_____

_____

_____

Have there been moments in your life when you felt like your voice was not heard or your truth was ignored? How did this affect your mental and emotional well-being?

_____

_____

_____

_____

Activity

Write letters to your younger self, acknowledging the pain and struggles you endured.

_____
_____
_____
_____
_____
_____
_____
_____
_____
_____
_____
_____
_____
_____
_____

Affirmation:
"I am ready to explore my consciousness and uncover the truths within."

And I Write...

Affirmation:
"I embrace the new dimensions of my life and the healing they bring."

And I Write...

Affirmation:
"I cherish genuine connections that provide solace and understanding."

CHAPTER TWO: Thirsty

Thirsty~DigginMyFlow What! I thirst?
Is there enough time?
Can this get any worse?
Write! I write. I love Spoken Word. SPEAK!
I RIGHT my way to freedom?
Close my eyes and envision the light.
The light at the end of the tunnel.
My writing - my CRE-A-SHON. I RIGHT my way to freedom!
Thirsty?
I want the truth on my way to the light. I WRITE!
Quench my tongue with truths
Through my teeth out it comes - The ROOT
I thirst!
My emotions! My energy!
I thirst!
Too much access to confusion.
My thoughts have allowed intrusion.
SPEAK to me and tell me the truth.
Where is my WELL?
Through spurts of Joy I cry.
In time all will tell.
Quench me.
Follow me.
I am on the right track.
Follow my tears and watch my inner heal.
Watch me deal. Cause every time is real.
You can't see my thoughts.
You can't hear me think.
From my own cup I DRINK.
I am drenched. My thirst is QUENCHED.

~and I write.
Jacqueline Gordon

More time to heal and explore your past

As you continue your healing journey, how do you quench your emotional thirst and what truths about your past do you feel ready to confront, accept, and release?

_____
_____
_____
_____
_____

What emotions come up as you think about releasing these truths?

_____
_____
_____
_____
_____

How do you think speaking and releasing these truths can help you move forward in your healing process?

_____
_____
_____
_____
_____

And I Write...

_____

_____

_____

_____

_____

_____

_____

_____

_____

_____

_____

_____

_____

_____

Affirmation:
"I honor my journey of self-discovery and acceptance. With each step forward, I courageously explore my past experiences with an open heart and mind. Through reflection and introspection, I embrace the truths of my healing journey, allowing myself to grow and evolve with compassion and grace."

And I Write...

Affirmation:
"My thirst for understanding is quenched through the depths of my emotions and creativity."

And I Write...

_____
_____
_____
_____
_____
_____
_____
_____
_____
_____
_____
_____
_____
_____
_____
_____

Affirmation:
"I am courageously embracing my journey of healing. With each step, I am reclaiming my voice, acknowledging my past, and nurturing my inner strength. I trust in the process of growth and transformation, knowing that I am worthy of love, understanding, and support."

Activity Instructions

Find a comfortable and quiet space where you can focus.

Reflect on your journey of exploring past trauma.

Use the space provided to create a visual representation of your thoughts and emotions related to your healing journey. You can draw, paint, or make a collage to express yourself.

Once you have completed your visual expression, take a moment to reflect on what you have created. Consider the symbolism and meaning behind each element of writing.

Write down your reflections in the spaces provided below your visual expression.

> **Our greatest glory
> is not in never
> falling,
> but in rising every
> time we fall.**
>
> – Nelson Mandela

CHAPTER THREE: Almost

Racing to the finish line,
walking faster than running with more time left behind.
But moving at a speed so right,
who would have thought I'd see the light?
Refueling my brain.
Keep it going. No! Stop moving. Back up quickly.
Now look? My mood's improving.
Trauma filled experiences you say?
My desire for my fearful thoughts to go astray.
Neither to be kept unconscious or hidden,
from reaching the finish line – now I am winning.
Move quicker than my eyes can see.
Touching and wrapping every emotion in me.
Craving and desperate, causing friction.
Running in place with no restrictions.
Rapidly I sprint for the cause.
Ready to seize this moment.
Who pressed pause?
Moving with no movement seen.
Based on fact or fiction.
Hell no this is not a dream.
Ready to beat this fear.
Run! Run! Run! And when you finish you scream!
Forget about the race.
Almost took my place.
On my knees behind the pew.
Underline fears for others to view.
Almost – to the finish line?
Swinging, sweating, betting that I beat the odds.
Crying, laughing, grabbing for my defenses.
Feeling like I've been robbed.
Today I ran a straight line.
Crossed over to the other side.
Trying – just trying to almost make my dreams come true.
No more time! No more fear!
Damn this pain! I am THROUGH.

~Jacqueline Gordon

"Almost" talks about "racing to the finish line." What is your own personal "finish line" when it comes to healing from your past? What does it look like, or how will you know you have reached it?

_____

_____

_____

_____

_____

_____

"Recall a time when you felt you were almost to the finish line, but encountered an obstacle. Describe this obstacle—it might be a feeling, an individual, or a situation.

_____

_____

_____

_____

The entry ends with a powerful declaration: "I am THROUGH!" What does "being through" mean to you? Is it about completely forgetting the pain, or is it about healing and moving through your life? Take a deep breath. Breathe...

_____

_____

_____

_____

Chapter 3 focuses on moving through the pain of trauma. While the finish line might seem distant, this chapter encourages you to acknowledge your progress and celebrate your victories, no matter how small. Now take a moment to reflect on the progress that you have made. How do you recognize and celebrate your victories?

_____

_____

_____

_____

_____

_____

_____

_____

_____

_____

_____

_____

_____

Activity

Developing a Mantra: A mantra is a word or phrase that can be repeated silently or aloud to focus your mind and bring a sense of calm. Think about a word or phrase that represents your strength, resilience, and hope for the future. Write it down and repeat it to yourself whenever you are feeling overwhelmed or discouraged.

___

___

___

___

___

___

___

___

___

___

___

___

Affirmation:
"I acknowledge my fears and face them with courage. I refuse to let past traumas dictate my future. Each day, I grow stronger and more resilient."

And I Write...

Affirmation:
"I live fully in the present, ready to seize every opportunity that comes my way. I do not let hesitation or doubt pause my progress. I am in control of my destiny."

Creating a Vision Board Instructions

A vision board is a powerful visualization tool that can help you manifest your goals and dreams. By surrounding yourself with images and words that represent your aspirations, you can inspire and motivate yourself to take action towards achieving them.

Collect magazines, newspapers, or printouts that you can use to cut out pictures or words that represent how you wish to be despite past trauma.

Use the space provided on the next page to cut out images and words that resonate with your aspirations. These could include images of things you want to achieve, places you want to visit, or the kind of person you aspire to be.

Arrange these images and words on the blank vision board template provided on the next page. Take your time to arrange and rearrange them until you are satisfied with the layout.

Once you have completed your vision board, cut out the vision board template page and find a place to hang it where you can see it every day —whether it is in your bedroom, office, or any other space where you spend time. Alternatively, you can take a picture of it and use the picture as your phone's wallpaper.

Affirmation:
"I am actively building a future free from the limitations of my past. Each step I take brings me closer to my dreams."

Vision Board Template

Visual Representation	Meaning

Take a few moments each day to look at your vision board and visualize yourself living your dreams.

Activity

Setting Healthy Boundaries

Instructions

Label the larger circle on the next page "Me" and the smaller circle "Others."

In your "Me" circle, take some time to reflect on your needs, values, and dealbreakers in relationships. These could include things like personal space, honesty, respect, or communication.

In your "Others" circle write out how you want other people to respect and interact with your boundaries. These might include behaviors and attitudes you expect from those you interact with.

Consider how these boundaries contribute to your overall well-being and sense of self in relationships.

Reflect on how you can communicate these boundaries effectively and assertively with others.

_____

_____

_____

_____

_____

Affirmation:
"I deserve respect and take care of myself by setting healthy boundaries. I speak up about what I need and build relationships that are based on respect and understanding."

In the Present Moment- Here and Now Free Zone

Can you recognize unhealthy patterns in your life? What are they?

_____
_____
_____

Are you able to set boundaries with others? How does this look?

_____
_____
_____

How can setting boundaries assist you in your healing?

_____
_____
_____

Have you ever felt like you had to sacrifice your own needs or well-being in a relationship, regardless of its nature because of your difficulty with setting boundaries?

_____
_____
_____

Reflect on how setting boundaries impacted your sense of self and your overall well-being.

_____

_____

_____

_____

_____

_____

_____

_____

_____

_____

_____

_____

_____

_____

_____

Affirmation:
"I push through pain and challenges, knowing they are temporary. I am determined, persistent, and capable of achieving my dreams. I will not be deterred by obstacles; I am victorious."

Affirmation:
"I move at my own pace, understanding that every step forward, no matter the speed, brings me closer to my goals. I cherish the journey and the growth it brings."

Creating a Support System

Think about the people in your life who are supportive, healthy, and respect your boundaries. Make a list of these people; they represent your support system. These are the people you can turn to for help and guidance as you move forward.

Instructions

In the boxes below, make a list of these people using an image or symbol that represents them.

Name	*Representation*

Name	Representation

Reflect on the qualities that make these individuals supportive and healthy influences in your life.

_____

_____

_____

_____

_____

_____

Consider how you can nurture and strengthen these relationships as you continue on your journey.

_____

_____

_____

_____

_____

_____

Affirmation:
Remember, these are the people you can turn to for help, guidance, and encouragement during your healing process.

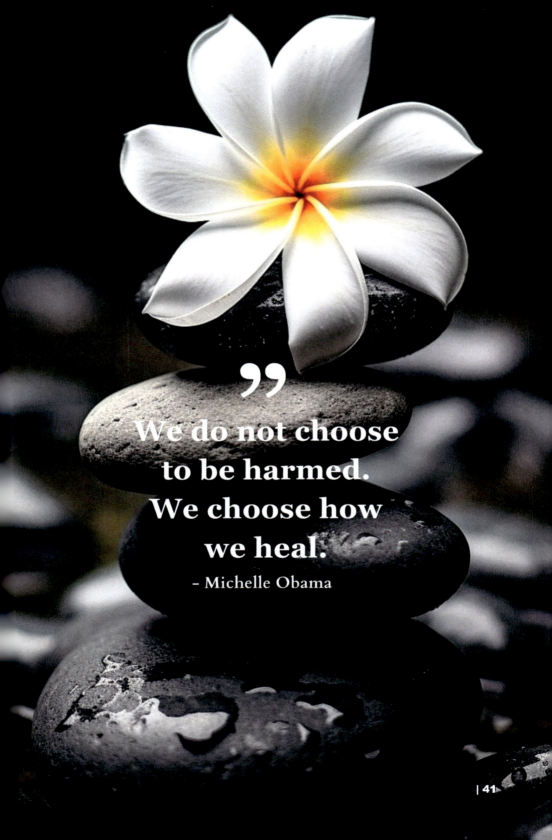

This section encourages you to let go of the past and focus on building a future filled with hope and possibility. Let's do this by reflecting on the following:

Reflect on how past experiences and memories have shaped your present emotions and behaviors.

_____

_____

_____

_____

What are some of the negative messages you tell yourself about your past experiences or your worthiness of love?

_____

_____

_____

_____

Are you holding on to painful memories?

Are these painful memories stopping you from moving forward in your healing process?

_____

_____

_____

_____

How do you reconcile the desire to hold on to cherished memories with the need to let go of painful ones?

_____

_____

_____

_____

Activities

In the space below, write down several things you are grateful for. These could be things like supportive friends or a beautiful sunset. Focusing on gratitude can help shift your perspective and cultivate a sense of optimism.

_____

_____

_____

_____

_____

_____

_____

_____

Affirmation:
"I am not defined by my past. I am choosing to heal, rewrite my story, and to let go of painful memories."

And I Write...

Affirmation:
"I trust the pace of my journey, knowing that every step forward is progress."

And I Write...

Affirmation:
"I confront my past with bravery, allowing myself to heal and move forward."

CHAPTER FOUR: Sadness

Sadness ought not be an emotional response to such a beautiful ending.
Quite frankly – it is not the end.
Even though this feeling
tends to drag my heart all over the place,
I'm chasing, and chasing, and chasing it but there is no race.

My heart.
It is heavy – chasing that drag to the end and longing for our connection to extend.
Ready? Or not! I cannot avoid the noise.

My mind is break-dancing in my head,
situating me away from the dread, my fear, my thoughts:
a kind of sadness that makes me wanna beg.

I'm a badass! Don't you know?
Then why the sadness?

I digress – not regress.
Just focus – focus on my growth.
Emotional ability – Emotional stability.
Create a dance for me to have both.

My oath - dance to the tune of reality's embrace.
In its rhythms, find your place.
It's not over, the story still untold,
in life's melody, a new chapter unfolds.

~Jacqueline Gordon

"Sadness" talks about the bittersweet nature of beautiful endings. This entry encourages you to embrace growth and find gratitude for the lessons learned, even as you prepare to let go.

The entry "Sadness" describes the heaviness of chasing closure and longing for a connection to extend. Have you ever experienced a similar heaviness in your own life when facing a beautiful, but sad ending?

_____
_____
_____
_____
_____
_____
_____
_____
_____
_____
_____
_____

Affirmation:
"I embrace the unknown future with excitement, knowing that my story is still unfolding and full of possibilities."

Activity

Take a moment to reflect on the depths of the emotions that are connected to a beautiful experience, but a sad ending.

_____

_____

_____

_____

_____

_____

_____

_____

_____

_____

_____

_____

_____

Affirmation:
"I am worthy of healing and closure. I am releasing the pain of the past and embracing the strength and resilience within me. I am moving forward with a lighter heart and an open mind."

And I Write...

Affirmation:
"I focus on my emotional growth and stability, understanding that I can handle my feelings with strength and grace."

And I Write...

Affirmation:
"I balance my emotions and thoughts, dancing to the rhythm of reality and finding my place in it."

CHAPTER FIVE: God's Grace

If I had one more chance to make all of my wrongs right,
I am so sure I wouldn't run out of time.
I would cherish the moments and all of the steps I took.
I wouldn't want this process to be a never-ending plight,
even for those who have already forgiven me.
Forgiveness is my birthright!

Who would not accept this offer?
And I get to do it at my own pace.
My first change would be the acknowledgment of God's Grace.
His free and unmerited favor.
I can remember the multitude of times He has thrown me a lifesaver.
And some of those times - believe it or not,
I took the credit. Yes! I took all of the credit.
How unthinking of me to not give God verbal and heartfelt merit?

So, to the people I was unkind to;
for the many times when I could have been more honest and true;
for the thoughts I created to support my displaced anger;
for the times I hated myself and took it out on a complete stranger;
for the times my family needed me, but my selfishness was more important;
for the thoughts that kept me looking at what you did to me and now those feelings lie dormant;
for the role I played in contributing to their grief and the looks on their faces in disbelief. Just to think of this makes me cringe.
I disappointed a lot of people and because of this, I offer my unlimited living amends.

God continues to bless me with His Grace,
sending Angels to my rescue – holding me in a safe place.
His unmerited favor and love,
I get that serene feeling on the inside and think to myself – this is truly some kind of divine spirit operating – regenerating and strengthening me

to be the very best person that I desire, more than ever to be.
I am living in a State of Grace.
The condition of being in God's Favor,
what a truly amazing gift from God
for me to savor.

~Jacqueline Gordon

Treat yourself with compassion, and acknowledge God's grace in your life. Then take a moment to reflect and write down your thoughts on the following:

What aspects of your past are you ready to let go of in terms of self-blame or guilt?

_____

_____

_____

_____

Can you identify specific ways you have contributed to your emotional pain?

_____

_____

_____

_____

What makes you deserving of unconditional love, grace, and healing?

_____

_____

_____

Write ways in which you have experienced God's grace at different points and stages of your life. Reflect on moments of unexpected blessings, guidance, and moments of divine intervention.

_____
_____
_____
_____
_____
_____
_____
_____
_____
_____
_____
_____
_____

Affirmation:
"I commit to being honest, kind, and true, making amends for past actions and striving to be the best version of myself."

Activity

In the space below, write a forgiveness letter to your present self. Express gratitude for your journey of healing and growth, and offer yourself forgiveness for any mistakes or shortcomings you may have experienced along the way. Affirm your worthiness of God's grace and love.

_____

_____

_____

_____

_____

_____

_____

_____

_____

_____

_____

_____

Affirmation:
"I let go of the past and embrace forgiveness as my birthright, allowing myself to heal and grow."

·And I Write...

_____
_____
_____
_____
_____
_____
_____
_____
_____
_____
_____
_____
_____
_____

Affirmation:
"I live in a state of grace, feeling strengthened and regenerated by the divine spirit, savoring the gift of God's love and favor."

And I Write...

Affirmation:
"With a grateful heart, I forgive myself and accept the divine light within me. I am bathed in grace, releasing the past and embracing a future filled with peace, a lighter heart, and an open mind to the future."

And I Write...

Affirmation:
"I commit to being honest, kind, and true, making amends for past actions and striving to be the best version of myself."

Throughout the day, practice acts of self-compassion and self-love. Treat yourself with gentleness and understanding, just as you would a dear friend. Engage in activities that bring you joy and nourish your soul, whether it is taking a walk in nature, practicing self-care, or spending time in quiet meditation and reflection. Remember that you are deserving of God's grace and love. Allow yourself to fully receive it as you continue on your journey of healing and growth.

Congratulations!

You have completed all five chapters of your healing journal. This is a significant accomplishment. Be proud of yourself for taking these steps toward healing and growth. Continue to practice self-care, reflect on your experiences, and embrace the concept of healing. You can move forward on your path to wholeness with time to spare and time to share. Live in the present and rewrite your life's story with healing and a beautiful beginning.

As you look back, re-read and process your thoughts about your writing. Remember that self-love is a powerful journey of healing and growth. It is a gentle and compassionate practice of embracing your true self, flaws and all. Through self-love, you can begin to unravel the knots of trauma that may have woven themselves into the fabric of your being. It is a process of reclaiming your worth, your voice, and your inner peace. Nurture yourself with kindness, understanding, and forgiveness. By doing so, you can gradually heal the wounds of the past and step into a brighter, more empowered future. Remember, you are worthy of love, healing, and happiness. Be gentle with yourself as you embark on this transformative journey of self-discovery and self-love.

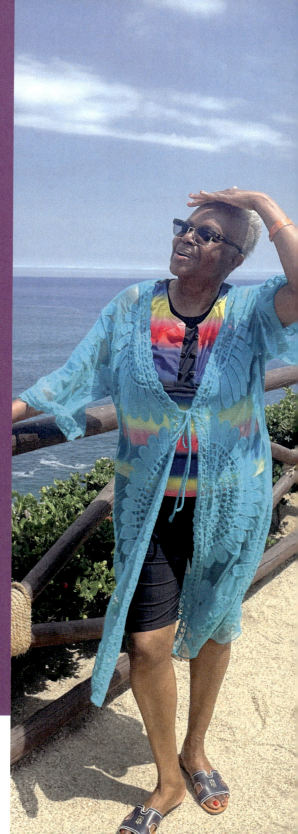

Echoes of the Soul

by

JACQUELINE GORDON

Made in the USA
Middletown, DE
05 July 2024